Mary Mary Quite Contrary
and
Hickory Dickory Dock

Illustrated by Nick Ward

Mary Mary Quite Contrary

Mary, Mary, quite contrary,
how does your garden grow?

With silver bells and cockle shells,
and pretty maids all in a row.

3

Hickory Dickory Dock

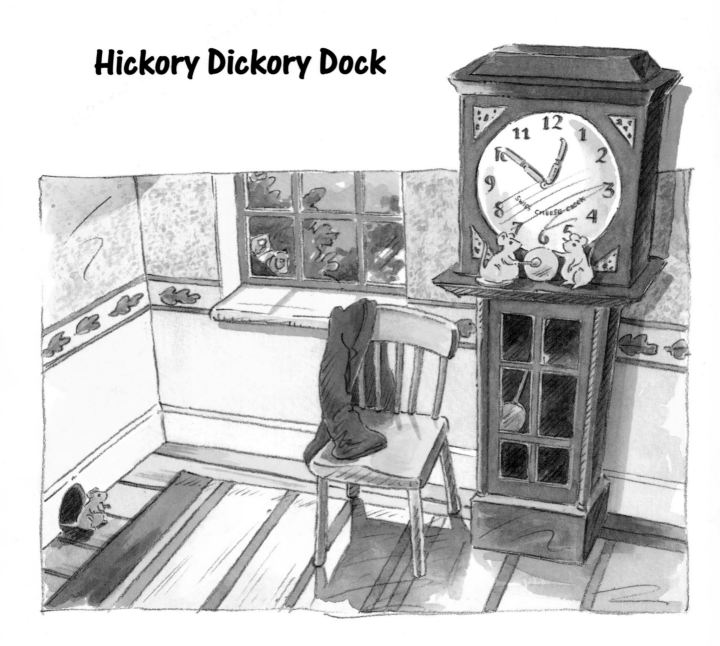

Hickory, dickory, dock.
The mouse ran up the clock.

The clock struck one.

The mouse ran down.
Hickory, dickory, dock.

Mary Mary Quite Contrary

Mary, Mary, quite contrary,
how does your garden grow?
With silver bells and cockle shells,
and pretty maids all in a row.

Hickory Dickory Dock

Hickory, dickory, dock.
The mouse ran up the clock.
The clock struck one.
The mouse ran down.
Hickory, dickory, dock.